KEEP IT SHUT

STUDY GUIDE

SIX SESSIONS STUDY GUIDE

KEEP IT SHUT

WHAT TO SAY, HOW TO SAY IT,
AND WHEN TO SAY NOTHING AT ALL

KAREN EHMAN

ZONDERVAN

Keep It Shut Study Guide
Copyright © 2014 by Karen Ehman

This title is also available as a Zondervan ebook. Visit www.zondervan.com/ebooks.

Requests for information should be addressed to:
Zondervan, 3900 *Sparks Dr. SE, Grand Rapids, Michigan* 49546

ISBN 978-0-310-81940-0

Cover design: Dual Identity
Cover illustrations: istockphoto®
Interior design: Katherine Lloyd, The DESK

First Printing November 2014 / Printed in the United States of America

CONTENTS

How to Use This Guide

Group Size

The *Keep It Shut* video curriculum is designed to be experienced in a group setting such as a Bible study, Sunday school class, or any small group gathering. After viewing each video together, members will participate in a group discussion. Ideally, discussion groups should be no larger than twelve people. You will notice occasional portions of the discussion where you are encouraged to break into smaller clusters of three to six people each for more heart-to-heart sharing and Scripture study. These times are clearly noted in the guide.

Materials Needed

Each participant should have her own study guide, which includes video outline notes, directions for activities, and discussion questions, as well as a reading plan and personal studies to deepen learning between sessions. Participants are also strongly encouraged to have a copy of the *Keep It Shut* book. Reading the book alongside the video curriculum provides even deeper insights that make the journey richer and more meaningful. (Also, a few of the questions pertain to material covered in the book.)

Timing

The time notations — for example (19 minutes) — indicate the *actual* time of video segments and the *suggested* time for each activity or discussion.
    For example:

Individual Activity: What Is God Saying to Me? (3 minutes)

Adhering to the suggested times will enable you to complete each session in about one hour. If you have additional time, you may wish to allow more time for discussion and activities, thereby expanding your group's meeting time to an hour and fifteen minutes or an hour and a half. If you are also having refreshments and a time of sharing prayer requests, figure another thirty minutes.

Facilitation

Each group should appoint a facilitator who is responsible for starting the video and keeping track of time during discussions and activities. Facilitators may also read questions aloud and monitor discussions, prompting participants to respond and ensuring that everyone has the opportunity to participate.

Between-Sessions Personal Study

Maximize the impact of the course with additional study between group sessions. Carving out about two hours total for personal study between meeting times will enable you to complete both the book and between-sessions studies by the end of the course. For each session, you may wish to complete the personal study all in one sitting or to spread it out over a few days (for example, working on it a half hour a day on four different days that week). PLEASE NOTE: If you are unable to finish (or even start!) your between-sessions personal study, still attend the group study video session. We are all busy and life happens. You are still wanted and welcome at class even if you don't have your "homework" done.

Scripture Memory

Each study includes a key Scripture verse that highlights the topic of the session theme. If you wish to maximize your learning experience, you may attempt to memorize these verses. In order to assist you with this goal, all six verses are printed in the back of the study guide.

You may photocopy this page on paper or card stock and then cut out the verses. (You really creative and crafty gals may even want to use scrapbooking paper to layer them on top of some decorative paper.) For your convenience, the memory verses are the size of a standard business card. You may wish to purchase a portable business card holder to keep them in. Then stash them in a handy place — perhaps your car, purse, or laptop bag. You can practice memorizing them while waiting in the car-pool line or at the doctor's office. Or you may wish to post them at your kitchen sink or on your bathroom mirror where you will see them each day. Laminating them will keep them from getting ruined if they get splashed.

It may be helpful to have the group facilitator inquire if any participants are attempting to memorize the key verses. Perhaps those members will want to show up five minutes early (or stay after for a few minutes) to practice reciting them to each other.

Bonus Session

Though there are only six sessions of video teaching, your group may desire to gather for one additional meeting — both to review the session six personal study section as well as to celebrate your time spent together during this curriculum. For your convenience, a seventh bonus session has been provided, featuring discussion questions, activities, and themed recipes should your group decide to serve a meal or refreshments.

Session 1

SPARKS, SQUABBLES, SPATS, AND SUCH: OUR WORDS MATTER

Death and life are in the power of the tongue,
and those who love it will eat its fruits.

(PROVERBS 18:21 ESV)

VIDEO: Sparks, Squabbles, Spats, and Such: Our Words Matter (19 minutes)

Play the video teaching segment for session one. As you watch, record any thoughts or concepts that stand out to you in the outline that follows.

Notes

Words are powerful and they have consequences.

What starts as a little spark can become a booming blaze, as in the Colorado Black Forest fire of 2013.

James 3:2–12 tells us this about the tongue:

- It can corrupt our whole body.

- It cannot be tamed.

- It cannot pour out both what is bitter and what is sweet.

Luke 6:45 states that the mouth speaks what the heart is already full of. We need to learn to "mind our spillage."

In our homes, often the problem isn't how we talk *about* our family members but rather how we talk *to* them.

Our tongues are fire. From where will they be lit: above or below? Are our words a sword or a salve?

Let's learn to pause before we pounce; to not say something permanently painful just because you are temporarily ticked off.

Perhaps we need a "force quit" feature for our mouths.

Group Discussion (10 minutes)

Take a few minutes to discuss what you just watched.

1. What part of the video teaching had the most impact on you?

2. Can you think of an example when, as a school-age girl, your words — or the words of one of your friends — caused drama? Describe the situation.

3. It has been estimated that women speak around twenty thousand words a day. That's a lot of yacking! Brainstorm as a group the many areas of life where we use our words — both spoken and written. Ready? Fire away.

Cluster Group Discussion (10 minutes)

If your group is comprised of more than twelve members, consider completing this discussion in smaller groups of three to six people each.

4. King David penned the words to Psalm 15. Have someone read this psalm aloud to the group. In the space below, record as many observations as you can about what is mentioned about our words. Number them as well to see how many you can come up with.

   • Our group's observations:

   • What do you learn from recording these particular words and phrases about the kind of person David says will "dwell on [God's] holy hill" (v. 1 ESV)?

   • Are there any guidelines you can draw out of this passage for how we can use our words wisely in the future? Can you think of a specific example that pertains to a current, real-life situation?

Group Discussion (15 minutes)

Gather back together as one large group and answer the following questions.

5. What is one insight you gained from the small group activity about Psalm 15 and the picture it paints of how we should use our words?

6. In the video segment, Karen described the Black Forest fire in Colorado in 2013. She also referred to James 3:2–6 and how in it James likens our tongue to fire. What insights did you get out of this analogy of fire? What similarities can you draw between the reality of fire and the effects of our words?

7. Karen talked about how her and her husband's opposite personalities and different styles of completing tasks can cause conflict and clashing. Do you live or work with someone who either has a polar opposite personality or does things in a way you never would? Does this ever make you use your words in a wrong manner? If so, how?

8. In the video, we were encouraged to "pause before we pounce" — to not say something permanently painful just because we are temporarily ticked off. Give an example of a time when you paused and it prevented you from wounding with your words, or a time when you didn't pause and you wish you had.

9. Time to flip your thinking! Instead of just "unloading" the next time you may be angry about someone's actions or irritated at the way he or she approaches situations, give yourself a little pep talk while you pause and ponder. List some things you might say to yourself to avoid saying something permanently painful just because you are temporarily ticked off.

10. "Are your words a sword or a salve?" Ouch! What does this word picture bring to mind when you read it? Can you think of anyone you know whose words seem to be a salve instead of a sword? Give an example. How do you feel when you are around them?

Individual Activity: What Is God Saying to Me? (3 minutes)

Complete this activity on your own.

Take a mental inventory of your life. In what areas do you most struggle with using your words correctly? It might not just be that you use them in an angry manner. It may be that you don't speak up when you should. Or you speak too much. Or you talk before really listening to the other person. Or you don't speak the truth because you are afraid of what someone else might think. Perhaps you are a people-pleaser and say yes when you should say no, and then find yourself overcommitted and miserable. Checkmark any areas below where you need a little help with your language:

- ❏ Work situations
- ❏ Relationship with my husband
- ❏ Relationship with my kids
- ❏ Dealing with neighbors
- ❏ Extended family situations
- ❏ When talking with other parents
- ❏ At church
- ❏ Online
- ❏ Friendships (either longtime friends or newer ones)
- ❏ When dealing with people I see throughout my day: at the grocery store, the bank, the coffeehouse, etc.
- ❏ Other _____

Now go back and put a star in front of the one or two areas where you most feel God may be prompting you to change how you behave when it comes to your speech.

Closing Prayer (2 minutes)

Have one person close in prayer. Then, get ready to learn more in your between-sessions personal study before meeting for session two!

BETWEEN-SESSIONS PERSONAL STUDY

Read and Learn

Read chapters 1–2 of the *Keep It Shut* book. Use the space below to record any insights you discovered or questions you may want to bring to the next group session.

Study and Reflect

1. Can you recall any incident from childhood or your teenage years where either you let your words get you in trouble, or the words of someone else stung so much that it still hurts somewhat (or even a lot!) today? What was it about the words spoken, or the person to whom they were said, that made this an incident you still can recall as an adult?

2. In chapter one of *Keep It Shut*, Karen writes this about James 3:6:

> The passage in James also talks about how the tongue can corrupt our whole body. I myself know very well from the times I have wished I could take back my words; often my whole body is affected. My mind races with regret. My heart pounds. My stomach churns and becomes tied up in knots as I fret and stress over what now might happen. My fingers fidget, and I can't seem to concentrate. Sometimes my feet pace as I ponder what I possibly can do now to get myself out of the royal mess I now find myself in.
>
> page 14

• Have you ever felt this way? If so, describe the situation here:

• How does this concept of our whole body being affected when we misuse our tongue tie into what James says in chapter 3, the last part of verse 2? Write what that portion of Scripture says here:

- The ESV and NIV versions of the Bible use the word *perfect* in James 3:2. The HCSB translation uses the word *mature*. The original Greek word used here is *teleios*. It is an adjective that means full-grown, complete, having reached maturity, especially as it relates to character. Does knowing the background of this word shed any new light on what you think this verse means?

- Finally, using a scale of 1 to 10 (with 1 being "never" and 10 being "always"), use the chart on the next pages to evaluate each relational area of your life when it comes to how often you speak in a mature manner, displaying character that is evidence of Christian growth. Record your rating in column two. Jot a phrase or two about what needs improvement (if anything) in column three. (You may need additional space if you have more family or work relationships than allowed for in the chart.)

Area	Rating	What I Need to Improve
Husband		
Child		
Child		
Child		
Child		
Child		
Family member		
Family member		
Family member		
Family member		
Coworker		
Coworker		

Area	Rating	What I Need to Improve
Coworker _____		
Friend _____		
Friend _____		
Friend _____		
Friend _____		
Online words (social media, blog comments)		
Church/civic situation		
Church/civic situation		
People in daily settings: bank, grocery store, etc.		
Other _____		
Other _____		
Other _____		
Other _____		

What do you learn from the preceding exercise? Do you see any commonalties?

A survey through the Bible reveals that God places great importance on the way we use our speech. In fact, the words *tongue, talk, speak, words, mouth,* and *silence* are used over 3,500 times in the Bible. The pages of Scripture are full of people just like you and me. Some of them serve as a great example of how we should use our words to build up, encourage, and speak for truth. However, there are others who seem to be the poster children for just how *not* to use our mouths.

Keep It Shut, pages 15–16

In chapter 2 of *Keep It Shut,* we encounter an example of someone who used his words — and sometimes his silence — wisely and strategically: the Old Testament character Joseph. Glance back over this portion in the book (pages 26 – 37), and then answer the following questions:

3. What stands out to you most about the way Joseph behaved when it comes to the words he uttered or even the times he remained silent? Did you learn anything new that you hadn't discovered about him before? If so, record it briefly in the space below.

4. Karen also listed several cues we can take from Joseph's life. Which most resonated with you? Checkmark any that apply and then, in the space provided, record why it jumped out at you. What is taking place in your life currently that made that particular statement speak to you right now?

√	Cue from Joseph's Life	Why It Speaks to Me
	Beware of bragging—and the impact your good news could have on others.	
	Say what honors God, not what other people want to hear.	
	Realize that lies are the minuscule snowflakes in a monumental snowball.	
	Give God credit where credit is due.	
	Watch your words in the workplace.	
	Just because you have a reason to retaliate does not mean you're justified in doing so.	
	Don't be God.	
	Do be nice.	

Now go back and place a star in front of the statement you most want to work on this next week. For added effect, write the statement on a sticky note and post it somewhere you will be sure to see it (your bathroom mirror, on your desk, on the dashboard of your car, etc.). Or set a calendar reminder on your phone for a few days from now with the particular phrase written out. When it pops up, do a quick self-evaluation to see how you are doing with regards to that principle from the life of Joseph.

> All the humans you encounter throughout the course of the day are "on purpose" people. God plopped them into your life for a reason.
>
> These souls — whether they are of the easy-to-love variety or the scratchy sandpaper kind — can be used by God to mold, reshape, and sometimes stretch our souls as he perpetually crafts us into creations who are becoming more and more like his Son.
>
> Will we be perfect?
>
> Nope. Never. (Not until heaven!)
>
> Just like Joseph?
>
> Maybe close.
>
> But of this I'm certain: others can catch a quick glimpse of Jesus when they see us speak and act in ways that honor him and line up with God's Word.
>
> *Keep It Shut*, page 41

5. In chapter 2 of *Keep It Shut* (pages 38–39), Karen explains the concept of grace and gracious speech as taught in the Bible. Does the clever way her husband was taught to remember just what grace is (G.R.A.C.E. = **G**od's **R**iches **A**t **C**hrist's **E**xpense) help your understanding? Or does it equip you to better explain it to someone else? How so?

6. Look up the following Bible passages. After each, write how it speaks to the concept of having gracious speech.

- Psalm 145:8

- Proverbs 15:26

- Proverbs 16:21

- Proverbs 16:24

- Ecclesiastes 10:12

- Colossians 4:6

X marks the spot! Based on what you just read in Scripture, how are you doing in the "gracious speech" quest? Place an X on the continuum below closest to where you would say your overall speech toward others generally falls:

```
├─────────────────────────┼─────────────────────────┤
```

Grumpy,   Usually gracious,   Gracious and godly ...
not very grace-giving   but I do have my moments   well, most of the time

Now, are there any adjustments you need to make to your language to enable your words to be more grace-laced? If so, what are they?

Scripture Memory Verse of the Week

Each week of this study will feature a verse to ponder and even memorize if you desire. For your convenience, all verses are printed in the back of this study guide. You may photocopy that page on card stock or colored paper and then cut out the verses to make them into memory cards. The memory verses are the size of a standard business card, so you can tuck them into a portable business card holder and carry them with you throughout the day. Or put them in a prominent place — purse, dashboard, desk, kitchen sink — where you can read, study, or memorize them. (You may want to laminate them if posting them at your kitchen sink. Karen has a friend who actually places laminated memory verses in her shower! She calls it her

"Showers of Blessing Prayer Closet.") Consider pairing with another study group member to help you stay accountable to memorize the six verses. You could come a few minutes early to class — or stay a bit longer — to practice your verses with each other.

Here is our verse for this week:

> *Hatred stirs up conflict, but love covers over all wrongs. Wisdom is found on the lips of the discerning.*
>
> Proverbs 10:12 – 13a

Session 2

ON FILLING GAPS AND ZIPPING LIPS: LISTEN TO OTHERS, TALK TO GOD

When there are many words, sin is unavoidable,
but the one who controls his lips is wise.

(PROVERBS 10:19 HCSB)

Checking In (10 minutes)

Welcome to session two of Keep It Shut. *An important part of this study is sharing what you have learned from reading the book and from completing your between-sessions personal study. Remember, don't worry if you weren't able to cover all the material. You are still welcome at the study and your input is valuable!*

- What from the session one video segment most challenged or encouraged you since the group last met together?

- What insights did you discover in reading chapters 1–2 of the *Keep It Shut* book?

- What stood out to you from the questions and activities in the between-sessions personal study?

VIDEO: On Filling Gaps and Zipping Lips: Listen to Others, Talk to God (18 minutes)

Play the video teaching segment for session two. As you watch, record any thoughts or concepts that stand out to you in the outline that follows.

Notes

Some people are verbal "gap fillers." When there is a break in the conversation, you can count on them to fill the slight gap of silence.

We sometimes suffer from FOMO (fear of missing out). We just have to say *something*!

The book of Proverbs can be considered the Twitter of the Old Testament. Tweets are short, pithy statements. Most proverbs are short and memorable pieces of biblical advice.

The advice of many proverbs "tweets" falls into the following four categories:

- *Don't speak too much.*
- *Don't speak too soon.*
- *Don't speak without first listening.*
- *Don't speak at all.*

If we suffer from FOMO and just have to keep talking to add our two cents' worth, saying, "But … but … but," we need to learn to "Shut the But" — shut it down!

Talking to God before we talk to others will allow the Holy Spirit to empower us to live life in a godly manner, processing as we pray. Then we are better able to break the habit of sinning with our mouths.

The Bible is full of examples of men and women who spoke filled with the Holy Spirit, some even when they were in a tight spot. When they did, Scripture never records them then sinning in what they said.

Group Discussion (10 minutes)

Take a few minutes to discuss what you just watched.

1. What part of the video teaching had the most impact on you?

2. Which of the four pieces of advice found in Proverbs — the Twitter of the Old Testament — did you most need to hear? (*Don't speak too much. Don't speak too soon. Don't speak without first listening. Don't speak at all.*) Don't share the why behind your choice just yet; you'll discuss that in a few minutes.

3. What thoughts do you have about our temptation to talk to others before we talk to God — hitting our phones or keyboards before we hit our knees? Can you relate? Has this ever gotten you into a mess?

Cluster Group Discussion (5 minutes)

If your group is comprised of more than twelve members, consider completing this discussion in smaller groups of three to six people each.

4. Do you remember anything about your school progress reports from growing up? Share any recollections with the group.

5. FOMO stands for "fear of missing out." For example, most teens fear missing out on fun. What do we women fear missing out on when it comes to conversations? Adding our opinion? Speaking words to clarify our position? Saying something funny to draw a laugh? Talk about what we fear missing out on.

Group Discussion (10 minutes)

Gather back together as one large group and answer the following questions.

6. Discuss your reactions to the following pieces of advice from Proverbs about using our words. As you work through each statement, explain why it is an admonition you need to hear. Is there a specific time recently, or even in the past, when you wish you had followed this advice? If you could rewind time, how would you handle the situation differently, using any of these principles?

    • *Don't speak too much.*

    • *Don't speak too soon.*

- *Don't speak without first listening.*

- *Don't speak at all.*

Assign the following verses to be read aloud by someone (or a few different people). After listening to each verse, take a moment to write out a summarizing statement that applies specifically to your life in the space below the verse. For example: Ephesians 4:26 declares, "In your anger do not sin." It could be summarized specifically by a stressed-out mom to read, "When my kids leave their toys out AGAIN — even though they've been told several times to put them away — it might make me angry, but I shouldn't let it make me sin by screaming at my kids." Ready?

- Proverbs 10:19

- Proverbs 29:20

- Proverbs 18:13

- Proverbs 17:28

- Proverbs 18:2

7. What is your normal default when it comes to processing life? Do you usually hit your knees before you hit the phone or head to the computer? If so, wonderful! If not, why do you think we sometimes reach out to others rather than run to God?

8. Have someone read Mark 13:11 aloud. True, we may never face persecution, but when we get into a tight spot verbally, we can learn to be quiet and enlist the help of the Holy Spirit before we use our words. Can you think of a situation where it would be beneficial for you to allow the Holy Spirit to tap on your heart and temper your words? If so, share it with the group.

Not only is it a bad habit to talk too much (and to talk before we really listen), but I have also discovered something else about my "Just-gotta-have-the-next-(and of course the last)-word" behavior. It often means this: not only am I not listening to the person I am with. I am also not listening to God.

Keep It Shut, page 57

Individual Activity: What Is God Saying to Me? (3 minutes)

Complete this activity on your own.

Has something during the time together today leapt off the page at you like a hyper grasshopper in the scorching heat of summer? Write out one concept or Scripture mentioned in the study that you feel the Holy Spirit may be prompting you to take note of.

What will you do differently now with regard to this idea?

Closing Prayer (2 minutes)

Have one person close the group in prayer. Then, get ready to learn more in your between-sessions personal study prior to session three!

BETWEEN-SESSIONS PERSONAL STUDY

Read and Learn

Read chapters 3–4 of the *Keep It Shut* book. Use the space below to record any insights you discovered or questions you may want to bring to the next group session.

Study and Reflect

1. Are you a gap-filler, jumping in verbally when there is a little lull in the conversation? List reasons you feel you sometimes do this. (If you aren't a major gap-filler, why do you think others who struggle with this issue try to fill the gaps of silence in a conversation?)

2. On page 48 of the book *Keep It Shut*, Karen lists four verses from Proverbs as Old Testament tweets. They are printed again here for your convenience. Circle the one that you think you need to remember most in your life right now.

   • "When there are many words, sin is unavoidable, but the one who controls his lips is wise." (10:19 HCSB)

   • "Do you see a man who speaks too soon? There is more hope for a fool than for him." (29:20 HCSB)

- "The one who gives an answer before he listens — this is foolishness and disgrace for him." (18:13 HCSB)

- "Even fools are thought wise if they keep silent, and discerning if they hold their tongues." (17:28)

Can you think of a specific reason or situation that prompted you to circle the verse that you did? Write that reason out here and include any change you would like to make in this situation as well.

> Has your mouth ever got you in trouble — yes, even made you sin — all because you talked too much? In your conversation you started to ramble. The more you spoke, the more your speech dug a deep hole, tripping you up and trapping you inside. Soon you were in a mighty tangled mess. It's certainly happened to me.
>
> *Keep It Shut*, page 49

3. In chapter 3 of *Keep It Shut*, Karen tells the story of talking to her friend at the basketball game. Because her "words were many," things got confusing and a conflict arose. Describe a situation in your life — either in the distant past or sometime more recent — when talking too much got you or someone you know into a heap of trouble.

Now, jot down a couple of sentences that you can use as go-to phrases when you know the conversation is heading south due to your excessive words. (Example: "I'm sorry. I'm talking too much. I'm gonna just hush up now.")

4. In chapter 4 of *Keep It Shut*, Karen tells about her college experience of trying to spend an hour in prayer. (That one didn't end well, did it?) Have you ever spent a long, concentrated time in prayer? Or do you find obstacles pop up that keep you from focusing and praying to God while all alone? In the space below, list what you think are your three greatest hindrances to spending time connecting with God through the practice of prayer.

    a.

    b.

    c.

Now, for each of the hindrances, list a possible solution in the lettered space below. If you have trouble coming up with a solution yourself, contact a trusted friend committed to the practice of prayer to see if she can offer any solutions.

a.

b.

c.

It has been said that if you fail to plan, you are planning to fail. That is an immensely accurate statement when it comes to the spiritual discipline of private prayer! In the space below, write out your game plan for the week when it comes to prayer. When will you pray? Where will you pray? How will you deal with distractions and possible interruptions? What tools will you use (your Bible, a journal, or perhaps a practical book on prayer)? Will you use some recorded music to sing praises to God?

Why, oh, why, is my default mode not to run to God first? To hit my knees *before* I hit the phone — or tap away on the keyboard? Though my natural inclination is to process *before* I pray, I am continually reminding myself to flip that script — with a sticky note posted near my kitchen sink and a screen saver on my phone, both sporting the same phrase — "But wait. Have you prayed about it?" We are better poised to process life's troubles after petitioning God first.

Keep It Shut, page 63

5. Take a few moments to review the account of Daniel that Karen covers in chapter 3 of *Keep It Shut* (pages 64 – 72). Which of these principles drawn from Daniel's life is one you most need to apply in your own life? Checkmark the one — okay, perhaps two — that you feel fit the bill.

   ❏ Surround yourself with like-minded friends.

   ❏ Watch your intake.

   ❏ Make prayer a daily priority.

   Why did you checkmark that particular statement? What do you feel God is saying to you about that principle? Do you need to make an adjustment in your thinking or your actions? If so, what is it?

Write a two- or three-sentence prayer to God about this topic. Openly pour your heart out to him, asking the Holy Spirit to guide and empower you to make the changes needed.

Scripture Memory Verse of the Week

Here is this week's verse to ponder, study, and even memorize if desired. (Remember, all the memory verses are printed together at the back of this study guide. You may photocopy them for your convenience.)

> *When there are many words, sin is unavoidable, but the one who controls his lips is wise.*
>
> Proverbs 10:19 HCSB

Session 3

OPINION-SLINGING AND SALTY SPEECH: ASSESSING OUR DIGITAL TONGUES

All a person's ways seem pure to them,
but motives are weighed by the LORD.

(PROVERBS 16:2)

Checking In (10 minutes)

Welcome to session three of Keep It Shut. *An important part of this study is sharing what you have learned from reading the book and from completing your between-sessions personal study. Remember; don't worry if you didn't get through all the material. You are still welcome at the study and your input is valuable!*

- What from the session two video segment most challenged or encouraged you since the group last met? Anyone have a chance to apply the advice in any of the Old Testament tweets we covered last time?

- What insights did you discover in reading chapters 3–4 of the *Keep It Shut* book? Share any particular favorites with the group.

- What did you find interesting or challenging in the between-sessions personal study questions?

VIDEO: Opinion-Slinging and Salty Speech: Assessing Our Digital Tongues (22 minutes)

Play the video segment for session three. As you watch, record any thoughts or concepts that stand out to you in the outline that follows.

Notes

There is a new national pastime these days: online opinion-slinging!

"I used to wish I could read minds. And then I got Facebook!"

Sometimes instead of being "friends" on social media, we have frenemies: someone who appears on the surface to be our friend, but stealthily, they are really an enemy.

Colossians 4:5–6 serves as a grid to run our words through before speaking them, especially online:

- Is this comment wise?

- Will writing this comment help me display God's love to outsiders?

- Is this comment full of grace?

- Is this comment seasoned with salt?

- Have I asked God if this is the best response?

In Matthew 5:13, Jesus tells believers that we are "the salt of the earth." What might this mean? Here are some facts about salt:

- Salt enhances flavor.
- Salt preserves.
- Salt is valuable.
- Salt purifies and softens.
- Salt melts hard ice.

When dealing with other people and wondering about their motives, believe the best before you assume the worst.

Our human default setting is to have hard hearts and thin skins. We need to flip that script and be tenderhearted and thick-skinned.

Group Discussion (10 minutes)

Take a few minutes to discuss what you just watched.

1. What part of the video teaching had the most impact on you?

2. What has been your experience with social media sites such as Facebook? Do you see people say things you doubt they'd say in person? Have you ever done so?

3. Have someone read Colossians 4:5–6 aloud. Of the questions in the video notes that Karen challenged us to ask ourselves when assessing our speech (all are based on this passage), is there one you hadn't thought of before? What thoughts do you have about this passage or these questions that you'd like to share with the group?

    • Is this comment wise?

    • Will writing this comment help me display God's love to outsiders?

- Is this comment full of grace?

- Is this comment seasoned with salt?

- Have I asked God if this is the best response?

4. Can you think of someone whose online speech you admire because it is full of grace? Tell the group about this person and what makes his or her online words stand out to you.

Cluster Group Discussion (10 minutes)

If your group is comprised of more than twelve members, consider completing this discussion in smaller groups of three to six people each.

5. The properties of salt covered in the video teaching or mentioned by Karen and Melissa in the wrap-up discussion are listed again below. As a group, come up with as many parallels to our words as you can. In short, how is each particular property of salt like our words when they are wise and gracious?

- Salt enhances flavor.

- Salt preserves.

- Salt is valuable.

- Salt purifies and softens.

- Salt melts hard ice.

- Salt prevents infection in a wound.

- Too much salt destroys the dish.

Can you think of a recent example where either your speech or the speech of someone else was salty? Which property showcased above did it display? Explain.

Of all the various properties of salt we have covered today, is there one God might be nudging you to notice? Example: Have your words not been soft toward someone online recently, and you need to remember that salty speech includes words that soften a situation?

Group Discussion (5 minutes)

Gather back together as one large group and answer the following questions.

6. Address the various properties of salt one by one, allowing each small group to report its findings.

7. Did you gain any new insight from this session's study of salt and its various characteristics? Share your favorite finding with the group and why you feel it most spoke to you. How can these observations help us when we use our words online?

Individual Activity: What Is God Saying to Me? (3 minutes)

Complete this activity on your own.

Ask God to bring to mind a time when you did *not* speak in a gracious or salty manner to someone online. Briefly describe the situation below. (You may wish to refrain from actually writing the person's name, using a code or cryptic initials instead.) If you can't think of an example of someone online, is there a family member, friend, or coworker who comes to mind instead?

Take a reflective moment to ask God if you need to go to this person to ask his or her forgiveness. If you believe the answer is yes, how will you do this? Jot down your plan here. Will you call? Send a handwritten letter? Meet in person?

Closing Prayer (2 minutes)

Have one person close the session in prayer. Don't forget to follow through on your plan from your individual activity. Then get ready for your between-sessions personal study prior to session four.

BETWEEN-SESSIONS PERSONAL STUDY:

Read and Learn

Read chapters 5–6 of the *Keep It Shut* book. Use the space below to record any insights you discovered, concepts that challenged you, or questions you may want to bring to the next group session.

Study and Reflect

1. In chapter 5 of *Keep It Shut*, Karen shared a story of her unkind words delivered with wrong motives to a woman who was at her home. Did this story spark a memory of when you said something that was technically true, but you said it with a wrong motive — in order to make someone else feel bad or guilty? Briefly describe the incident.

2. Read Proverbs 16:2 in as many Bible versions as you can find. (You may want to use an online source such as BibleGateway.com.) Then, in the space provided, summarize this verse in a sentence that is applicable and memorable to you.

If we want to become people who not only utter words that are true but also say them for the right reasons, what are we to do? How do we train our brains and tame our tongues in order to make sure that our motives and manners line up with God's Word? Whenever I need practical wisdom like this, one of the first places I look for answers is the book of Proverbs.

Keep It Shut, page 81

3. For each of the following pairs of statements, circle the one that best describes your manners and motives when dealing with the people with whom you spend the most time. (It may be family members, roommates, or even coworkers.)

I usually don't speak until I believe I have all of the facts straight.	I often speak without all of the necessary information about a situation.
Usually my goal truly is to help another person with my words, regardless of whether he or she has hurt me in the past.	Sometimes my goal is to put a little pinch in another person's heart because he or she has done something that has made me angry.
I steer clear of saying things that will make me look good because I don't want to appear to be bragging.	I sometimes work my words in such a way that it makes me look better than I really am.
I am careful to only speak words of correction to someone with whom I have a solid and trusting relationship.	I sometimes correct or instruct people whom I don't know well or have a close friendship with.
I keep quiet and pray for others, asking the Holy Spirit to speak to them.	I sometimes try to play Holy Spirit by strongly suggesting or even telling others what to do.

4. What are some internal cues in your heart and mind that might alert
    you to the fact that your motives may be wrong? What can you do in
    the future when you start to feel your heart slipping into a place of
    wrong motives?

Karen said in the video: "Our human default setting is to have hard
hearts and thin skins. We need to flip that script and be tenderhearted
and thick-skinned." While we should be careful to examine our own
motives closely — making sure we aren't trying to poke a hole in
someone's happiness or make another person feel bad — we shouldn't
always jump to conclusions about the motives of others. Can you
think of an example from your life when you were thin-skinned (let
an offense rattle you) and it hardened your heart? How might possess-
ing thick skin in that situation instead have led to a tender heart?

Then there's that aspect of *sly* defined as being *lightly* mischievous. The word *lightly* sheds a whole new light on the
topic of mischievousness. It's not like I am trying to be all-
out dishonest or disruptive. I am only slightly off course. Just
a tiny bit dishonest or a tad bit mischievous. But as I often
tell my children, a half-truth is still a whole lie. And a slam,
whether overt or subtle, is still a slam.

Keep It Shut, page 85

5. On a scale of 1 to 10 (1 meaning "never" and 10 meaning "always"), when it comes to how often you usually believe the best about someone instead of assuming the worst, where would you honestly say you fall in the following relationships?

I believe the best before I assume the worst about my spouse's behavior.

1	2	3	4	5	6	7	8	9	10

Never   Always

I believe the best before I assume the worst about my children's behavior.

1	2	3	4	5	6	7	8	9	10

Never   Always

I believe the best before I assume the worst about my boss's behavior.

1	2	3	4	5	6	7	8	9	10

Never   Always

I believe the best before I assume the worst about my extended family members' behavior.

1	2	3	4	5	6	7	8	9	10

Never   Always

I believe the best before I assume the worst about my friends' behavior.

1	2	3	4	5	6	7	8	9	10

Never   Always

6. What do you discover as you review the continuums from question 5? Are there some people in your life who are easier to believe the best about? Why do you think you assume the worst about others? Perhaps there is a legitimate reason due to past history, but how can you wipe the slate clean and avoid making assumptions each time you interact with them?

Are there any changes you would like to make when it comes to jumping to conclusions about the motives of others?

Women today have a unique challenge of not only having to watch the words that tumble out of our mouths but also the ones that we type with our manicured fingertips. Time to talk about our digital tongues!

7. For each of the following statements, circle the corresponding phrase that applies.

I spend time each day on the Internet or social media sites.

"Never, ever!"   "Once in a great while."   "Okay, I do this sometimes."   "Yeppers. This describes me often."   "Yikes! I do this a lot."

I enjoy "liking" posts, leaving comments on blogs, or replying to what others have written online.

"Never, ever!"   "Once in a great while."   "Okay, I do this sometimes."   "Yeppers. This describes me often."   "Yikes! I do this a lot."

I enjoy posting and sharing my own thoughts online or on my social media accounts.

"Never, ever!"   "Once in a great while."   "Okay, I do this sometimes."   "Yeppers. This describes me often."   "Yikes! I do this a lot."

I say things privately online to someone that I probably would not say in person.

"Never, ever!"   "Once in a great while."   "Okay, I do this sometimes."   "Yeppers. This describes me often."   "Yikes! I do this a lot."

I type words publicly online that I probably wouldn't say to someone's face.

"Never, ever!"   "Once in a great while."   "Okay, I do this sometimes."   "Yeppers. This describes me often."   "Yikes! I do this a lot."

I type a comment or thought online but then delete it before actually posting it because I am convicted it is wrong, or I am afraid it might look unkind.

"Never, ever!"   "Once in a great while."   "Okay, I do this sometimes."   "Yeppers. This describes me often."   "Yikes! I do this a lot."

*I have had to delete Facebook comments, tweets, or other content
I have put up online because I become convinced I shouldn't
have said it in the first place.*

"Never, ever!"   "Once in a great
while."   "Okay, I do this
sometimes."   "Yeppers. This
describes me often."   "Yikes! I do
this a lot."

*I participate in online "fights" where people are commenting
back and forth about an issue, opinion, or person.*

"Never, ever!"   "Once in a great
while."   "Okay, I do this
sometimes."   "Yeppers. This
describes me often."   "Yikes! I do
this a lot."

Look back over the preceding exercise. What do you discover about your digital tongue? Do you see any patterns? Any concerns? Any changes that need to be made? In two or three sentences, write what you sense God is teaching you about this important and very public part of our relationships in today's culture.

8. Reread the section of chapter 6 in *Keep It Shut* about the various properties of salt (pages 106–110). You covered the characteristics of this common household seasoning in the group session, and they are repeated below for your convenience. Circle your favorite finding and then write a few sentences about why it's meaningful to you.

   • Salt enhances flavor.

- Salt preserves.

- Salt is valuable.

- Salt purifies and softens.

- Salt melts hard ice.

- Salt prevents infection in a wound.

- Too much salt destroys the dish.

Scripture Memory Verse of the Week

Here is this week's verse to ponder, study, and even memorize if desired. Or because we studied about the words we speak online, perhaps you will want to post this one on your computer screen. (Remember, all the memory verses are printed in the back of this study guide. You may photocopy them for your convenience.)

> *My mouth speaks what is true, for my lips detest wickedness.*
> *All the words of my mouth are just; none of them is crooked*
> *or perverse.*

Proverbs 8:7–8

Session 4

GOSSIP, FLATTERY, AND PEOPLE-PLEASING: HOW TO SPEAK THE TRUTH IN LOVE

They have become filled with every kind of wickedness, evil, greed and depravity. They are full of envy, murder, strife, deceit and malice. They are gossips.

(ROMANS 1:29)

Checking In (10 minutes)

Welcome to session four of Keep It Shut. *An important part of this study is sharing what you have learned from reading the book and from completing your between-sessions personal study. Remember, don't worry if you didn't get through all the material. You are still welcome at the study and your input is valuable!*

- What from the session three video teaching most challenged or encouraged you since the group last met? Did you notice any difference in the words you used while online?

- What insights did you discover from reading chapters 5–6 of the *Keep It Shut* book?

- What most spoke to you from the between-sessions personal study questions?

VIDEO: Gossip, Flattery, and People-Pleasing: How to Speak the Truth in Love (22 minutes)

Play the video segment for session four. As you watch, record any thoughts or concepts that stand out to you in the outline that follows.

Notes

"If you haven't got anything nice to say about anybody, come sit next to me." — Alice Roosevelt, President Teddy Roosevelt's daughter

"He who gossips with you will also gossip about you." — An old Irish proverb

Gossiping isn't just a personality trait. It is a sin.

In Scripture, the word *sin* was originally used by archers of arrows that "missed the mark." Anything other than dead center bull's-eye is sin. Romans 1:29–32 lists many sins, such as murder and envy. It also mentions gossiping.

Sticks and stones may break my bones, but words can never hurt me? No! Bruises fade and bones heal, but a scorched heart may take years to mend.

So, what do we do to stop gossiping?

- Adopt the reverse Nike slogan, "Just DON'T do it!"

- Know when to eat your words and admit your fault. (see Proverbs 6:1 – 5)

- Make a promise to yourself and to others.

- Remember, the closest exit may be somewhere behind you.

It has been said that gossip is saying something behind someone's back that you would never dare say to the person's face. However, flattery is almost the opposite. It is saying something to someone's face that you would probably never say behind his or her back.

Herod Antipas was struck with the disease to please. Because of his oath and his dinner guests, John the Baptist ended up getting beheaded.

Group Discussion (10 minutes)

Take a few minutes to discuss what you just watched.

1. What part of the teaching had the most impact on you? Any *Hee Haw* fans in the room? If so, for fun, what was your favorite part of the show?

2. What are your thoughts about the word *gossip* being listed alongside other sins usually thought of as serious (greed, murder, and malice) in Romans 1:29–32?

3. Do you, like King Herod, ever struggle with people-pleasing? How so? Do you say flattering things to people? Or do you say yes to things you wish you had said no to and now you feel overcommitted? Do you sometimes even shade the truth in order to not hurt someone's feelings or to be liked? As a group, brainstorm as many reasons as you can why we sometimes suffer from the disease to please.

> We must not confuse the command to love with the disease to please.
>
> Lysa TerKeurst, *The Best Yes*, page 5

Cluster Group Discussion (10 minutes)

If your group is comprised of more than twelve members, consider completing this discussion in smaller groups of three to six people each.

4. Have a person read aloud the following verses one at a time. After each verse is read, discuss what you learn about gossip from the verse. Record your findings in the spaces provided:

    - Proverbs 11:13

    - Proverbs 16:28

    - Proverbs 20:19

    - Proverbs 26:22

    - 2 Corinthians 12:20

    - Proverbs 26:20

    Which of the preceding verses most challenged or convicted you? Can you share the reason why?

If you were going to pick one of the verses about gossip to memorize, which one would it be?

For the brave and ambitious: Exchange cell phone numbers with someone else in your group who might also want to memorize one of the verses. Text each other throughout the week to see how your memorization is coming, or talk on the phone and practice the memory verse aloud. Then next week when you get together, try to recite the verse from memory with your study partner.

Group Discussion (5 minutes)

5. Have the cluster groups take turns summarizing what they discovered from the verses about gossip. How many in the group decided to take on the memory verse challenge with a partner?

6. In the video session, Karen told the story of being on an airplane and hearing the flight attendant say, "Remember, the closest exit may be somewhere behind you." What do you think of the idea of approaching someone from your past whom you wounded with your words, or about whom you gossiped, and asking for forgiveness? Have any of you ever done this or had it done to you? Share your experience with the group if you can, being careful not to use specific names or other identifying/confidential details.

Individual Activity: What Is God Saying to Me? (3 minutes)

Ask God to bring to mind a situation where you either used gossip, hearsay, flattery, or people-pleasing. Record that situation briefly here in the space provided.

Now write a prayer — speaking to God with all honesty — about this situation. Ask him to whisper to your heart and impress on your mind exactly what action you should take about this relationship in your life.

Closing Prayer (2 minutes)

Have one person close the session in prayer. Then get ready for your between-sessions personal study time prior to the next meeting.

BETWEEN-SESSIONS PERSONAL STUDY

Read and Learn

Read chapters 7–8 of the *Keep It Shut* book. Use the space below to record any insights you discovered or questions you may want to bring to the next group session.

Study and Reflect

1. No doubt every person doing this study has either been the victim of gossip or has at least one time in her life gossiped about someone else. Most likely both scenarios are true. When you ponder either the times that you have participated in gossip or were the object of it, which situations pop into your mind? Briefly jot the details here, along with the time frame when it took place.

   If you could revisit the situations you just described, how would you handle things differently? What choices could you have made that would have prevented you from gossiping, or what actions would you have taken when you were being gossiped about?

2. In chapter 7 of the book *Keep It Shut,* Karen mentions our tendency in Christian circles to participate in gossip but cloak it as a prayer request. Be honest. Have you ever done this? If so, when? What guidelines could you implement in order to ensure that — even if you are sincerely asking for prayer — the words you speak are not gossip. List those guidelines here.

> The word *gossip* appears at least a dozen times in both the Old and New Testaments. The Old Testament Hebrew word is *rakil,* which refers to one who travels about speaking slander or telling tales. The New Testament Greek word is *psithurismos,* which describes a whisperer who goes around revealing secrets in order to paint someone else in a bad light. Throughout the Bible, a gossip is never spoken of highly. Gossip is always treated as something that does damage and is to be avoided.
>
> *Keep It Shut,* page 118

3. In chapter 7 of *Keep It Shut* (pages 117–118), Karen outlines what she feels are examples of what gossip is and also what gossip is not. Choose one statement from each list — both what gossip is and what it is not — that most jumped out at you when you read it. Write those two statements below, and after each, explain why you selected it. Can you think of more examples that fit either category?

4. Take a couple of minutes to read Psalm 31, printed on the next two pages. As you do, mark it in the following way:

   • Circle any references to people who were either talking about David or plotting and scheming against him.

   • Draw a box around any verses that mention what David is thinking or feeling or what action he is taking or will take.

   • Place a star next to any verses that tell what God is doing or thinking during this incident in David's life.

   • Go back and put a ☺ next to your favorite verse or section of this psalm.

   • NOTE: You may also use three different colored highlighters for the three different marks.

   After you have finished: What has this little markup exercise taught you? What principles can you draw from Psalm 31 when you are facing enemies or are the victim of gossip?

Psalm 31

[1] In you, LORD, I have taken refuge; let me never be put to shame; deliver me in your righteousness.

[2] Turn your ear to me, come quickly to my rescue; be my rock of refuge, a strong fortress to save me.

[3] Since you are my rock and my fortress, for the sake of your name lead and guide me.

[4] Keep me free from the trap that is set for me, for you are my refuge.

[5] Into your hands I commit my spirit; deliver me, LORD, my faithful God.

[6] I hate those who cling to worthless idols; as for me, I trust in the LORD.

[7] I will be glad and rejoice in your love, for you saw my affliction and knew the anguish of my soul.

[8] You have not given me into the hands of the enemy but have set my feet in a spacious place.

[9] Be merciful to me, LORD, for I am in distress; my eyes grow weak with sorrow, my soul and body with grief.

[10] My life is consumed by anguish and my years by groaning; my strength fails because of my affliction, and my bones grow weak.

[11] Because of all my enemies, I am the utter contempt of my neighbors and an object of dread to my closest friends — those who see me on the street flee from me.

(cont.)

¹² I am forgotten as though I were dead; I have become like broken pottery.

¹³ For I hear many whispering, "Terror on every side!" They conspire against me and plot to take my life.

¹⁴ But I trust in you, LORD; I say, "You are my God."

¹⁵ My times are in your hands; deliver me from the hands of my enemies, from those who pursue me.

¹⁶ Let your face shine on your servant; save me in your unfailing love.

¹⁷ Let me not be put to shame, LORD, for I have cried out to you; but let the wicked be put to shame and be silent in the realm of the dead.

¹⁸ Let their lying lips be silenced, for with pride and contempt they speak arrogantly against the righteous.

¹⁹ How abundant are the good things that you have stored up for those who fear you, that you bestow in the sight of all, on those who take refuge in you.

²⁰ In the shelter of your presence you hide them from all human intrigues; you keep them safe in your dwelling from accusing tongues.

²¹ Praise be to the LORD, for he showed me the wonders of his love when I was in a city under siege.

²² In my alarm I said, "I am cut off from your sight!" Yet you heard my cry for mercy when I called to you for help.

²³ Love the LORD, all his faithful people! The LORD preserves those who are true to him, but the proud he pays back in full.

²⁴ Be strong and take heart, all you who hope in the LORD.

However, neither stuff nor status holds the key to our happiness. The key is in our stance before God. David states, "I will be glad and rejoice in your unfailing love, for you have seen my troubles, and you care about the anguish of my soul" (Psalm 31:7 NLT). David realized that his joy could only come from his relationship with God, from knowing that he was utterly and fully loved. Loved with a love that would never fail. Never. *Ever.* Even when his enemies were pressing hard on every side tossing out accusations and hurling hateful words, David could still strike a vein of joy when he fixed his focus on God.

Keep It Shut, page 124

5. Read Psalm 141:3, and then write this verse below in your own sweet handwriting:

In chapter 7 of *Keep It Shut,* Karen mentioned Psalm 141:3 when she spoke of making a commitment to her friend not to talk about the situation that was happening with her family member. What do you think of making such a promise to someone?

Is there a person in your life right now who might be blessed by such a commitment from you?

Describe how you would feel if someone were to pledge to you this promise.

> How about we try to tie our tongues a little more frequently in the future? Knowing how devastating repeating hearsay and speaking words of gossip can be should keep us from participating in this verbal form of destruction. Instead of a little three-point checklist, how about we tape this up next to our kitchen sink instead:
>
> I can *hear* you.
> Love, God
>
> *Keep It Shut*, page 133

6. Ecclesiastes 5:2 urges us, "Do not be quick with your mouth, do not be hasty in your heart to utter anything before God. God is in heaven and you are on earth, so let your words be few." How does this verse related to the subject of people-pleasing? Can letting "your words be few" help avoid the trap of flattery and people-pleasing? How so?

7. Read Psalm 15 slowly. Then, read it through once more and write out the actions listed in this Scripture of the person who may "dwell" with God and "never be shaken." Also, list the verse where you found the action mentioned. The first one has been done for you.

Verse:	Action:
2	*They walk in a way that is blameless.*

Scripture Memory Verse of the Week

Here is this week's verse to ponder, study, and even memorize if desired. (Remember, all the memory verses are printed together at the back of this study guide. You may photocopy them for your convenience.)

> *Instead, we will speak the truth in love, growing in every way more and more like Christ, who is the head of his body, the church.*
>
> Ephesians 4:15 NLT

Session 5

PAUSE BEFORE YOU POUNCE: ON CULTIVATING SOFT SPEECH

My dear brothers and sisters, take note of this:
Everyone should be quick to listen, slow to speak
and slow to become angry, because human anger
does not produce the righteousness that God desires.

(JAMES 1:19 – 20)

Checking In (10 minutes)

Welcome to session five of Keep It Shut. *An important part of this study is sharing what you have learned from reading the book and from completing your between-sessions personal study. Remember, you are still welcome at the study even if you weren't able to complete the material.*

- Think back to the session four video segment you viewed last time. Is there anything that comes to your mind as memorable when you think of that session?

- What insights did you discover from reading chapters 7–8 of the *Keep It Shut* book?

- What most jumped out at you from the between-sessions personal study?

- Do you have any questions for the group?

VIDEO: Pause Before You Pounce: On Cultivating Soft Speech (23 minutes)

Play the video segment for session five. As you watch, record any thoughts or concepts that stand out to you in the outline that follows.

Notes

When the actions of others threatened to make us angry, we need to learn to mind our own sin.

James 1:19–20 urges us to be quick to listen, slow to speak, and slow to become angry because our anger does not produce the righteousness that God desires. However our natural tendency is to be slow to listen, quick to speak, and faster than Usain Bolt to become angry! (If you don't know who he is, Google him!)

Ephesians 4:26–27 instructs us: "'In your anger do not sin': Do not let the sun go down while you are still angry, and do not give the devil a foothold." We can observe four principles from this passage:

- First, we are going to get angry.

- We should not sin. (Learn to attack the problem, not the person.)

- We need to deal with our anger, and PRONTO! (The longer we stew, the more likely we are to strike.)

- Finally, beware of the Devil's sneaky wrestling moves. He wants to get a foothold.

Proverbs 15:1 says, "A soft answer turns away wrath, but a harsh word stirs up anger" (ESV). We need to learn to give a soft — even Snuggie®-like — answer!

Giving a soft answer doesn't mean I don't give a truthful one.

Don't be a gasoline queen, throwing fuel on a small spark that could ignite a fiery feud.

Before interacting with others, sometimes — in a spiritual sense — we need to utter the words Karen's son spoke when playing with his video game: "Hang on a second. I gotta die." We must learn to embrace and adopt the practice the apostle Paul mentions in 1 Corinthians 15:31, "I die daily."

Group Discussion (10 minutes)

Take a few minutes to discuss what you just watched.

1. What part of the teaching had the most impact on you?

2. Can you relate to the story of the scattered shoes in Karen's garage? Are there times when the people in your home or at work or another relational situation do things that tempt you to blow your stack?

   Can you think of an example from your own life when someone else acted wrongly (or your kids didn't do what you asked them to) and it enticed you to sin as well? How can the concept of "minding your own sin" help you to choose a different course of action the next time you bump into this same situation or one like it?

3. Have someone read James 1:19–20 aloud. Then write the three commands given there in the space below. (Most Bible versions say, "quick to listen, slow to speak and slow to become angry." However, the one read to your group may word them differently.)

   Now as a group, practice saying these commands out loud. You may look down at your study guide the first few times. Then try to say them from memory.

Which of these commands is most difficult for you? Why do you think that's so?

Cluster Group Discussion (8 minutes)

If your group is comprised of more than twelve members, consider completing this discussion in smaller groups of three to six people each.

4. Have one person read aloud Ephesians 4:26–27 in as many versions of the Bible as you have available. (Use an app on a smartphone, if you wish.)

    Does anyone have a story to share of a time when you *did* let the sun go down on your anger and gave the Devil a foothold (in some versions "an opportunity")? Be careful not to share names and details so as to break a confidence or cast blame on someone.

    Time to take the truths of Scripture and wrap them around the realities of life! How specifically can the instructions in this passage help you to be angry but not sin? In short, how can containing your anger and not letting it lead to sinful behavior (dealing with it quickly) prevent Satan from getting a foothold not only on the situation but ultimately on your heart, actions, and reactions?

Group Discussion (7 minutes)

5. Have the cluster groups share one insight from their discussion of Ephesians 4:26–27.

6. In the video session, Karen mentioned that giving a soft answer is like wrapping up someone in a Snuggie® — calm, warm, and comforting. Why do you think it is hard to speak softly but easy to be short, snippy, or even snarky when answering someone's repeated or somewhat annoying question?

7. How can the picture that's painted in Proverbs 15:1 help you to change your behavior when answering someone else? What can you do to remind yourself that the Bible wants us to answer softly? Any tips for the group?

8. What do you think of the concept of laying down our lives for others not just meaning we are willing to die in their place but also daily dying to ourselves by putting them first? (That includes gathering our composure before we interact with them so we do so in a kind manner.) Discuss your reaction to the story of Karen's son and his video game, especially his phrase, "Hang on a second. I gotta die."

Individual Activity: What Is God Saying to Me? (3 minutes)

Take a moment to get alone with your thoughts, quiet before the Lord. Ask him to reveal the one area in your life where you most struggle with speaking harshly, being quick to get angry, or letting your annoyance lead to sin. Write briefly about it here.

Now, in your own sweet handwriting, copy the phrase below that is strategically stitched inside James 1:19. BUT don't put a period at the end of the sentence. Instead, add the words "even when it comes to" and then craft a phrase about the situation you just wrote about above to finish your sentence.

Everyone should be quick to listen, slow to speak and slow to become angry . . .

Closing Prayer (2 minutes)

Have one person close the session in prayer. The next time the group meets will be the final teaching segment. Boo! Are you already tearing up? Enjoy your time between sessions.

BETWEEN-SESSIONS PERSONAL STUDY

Read and Learn

Read chapter 9 of the *Keep It Shut* book and record any thoughts or insights you discovered in the space provided.

Study and Reflect

> Will you commit with me to answering annoying questions in a soft and gentle way? To refuse to throw gasoline on a small spark that could ignite a fiery family feud or cause a ruckus with your coworkers? Will you work to defuse the fight before it even begins? Your family and friends might notice your effort and reward you by responding in kind. (Or maybe by even buying you your very own Snuggie®!)
>
> *Keep It Shut*, page 164

1. In chapter 9 of *Keep It Shut*, Karen recalls how her friend's daughter once scribbled with permanent marker all over the Ehmans' newly purchased children's plastic picnic table. Though Karen held it together and didn't use an angry tone with the young doodler, it might not have been the same scenario if one of her own dear darlings had played Picasso with that picnic table! Why do you think it is easier for us to control our tempers — and our tongues — with those outside our immediate family?

What little pep talk can you give yourself about how this reality should not be? Write your thoughts here.

2. Read the following verses and record your thoughts about the light they shed on anger. The list is long, but don't hurry through it. Split these questions over two or three days if you need to in order to let the full weight of each verse sink into your heart and solidify in your mind.

- Psalm 37:8

- Proverbs 22:24

- Proverbs 30:33

- Ecclesiastes 7:9

- 1 Corinthians 13:4–6

- Ephesians 4:31–32

- Colossians 3:8

- Proverbs 29:22

- Ecclesiastes 5:6 (the first sentence of the verse)

- Matthew 5:22

- Proverbs 15:18

- Proverbs 17:14

- Proverbs 17:19 (OUCH!)

Now how would you summarize in your own words what the Bible teaches on anger, based on the verses you just studied? It doesn't have to be an exhaustive paragraph, just a few simple sentences that highlight the principles that most leapt out at you as you pondered them.

Anger is inevitable. People are going to push your buttons — and you are going to push back. Or maybe their intent wasn't to tick you off, but you are hoppin' mad anyway. You hope to respond in a way that lines up with God's Word. But when you don't, and instead dwell on the offense, letting bitterness begin to boil up inside, you must address your anger — and fast! I know this from experience: the longer you stew, the more likely you are to strike. No wonder the Bible advises us to deal with anger promptly.

Keep It Shut, page 160

3. Have you ever been guilty of being a "gasoline queen" — of drizzling or even dousing gasoline on an already heated conversation, making it even worse? If you can recall such a time, jot the details of it briefly here.

In retrospect, and based on what you have learned in this week's study, how could you do things differently the next time a slightly heated conversation is beginning to combust and flare, threatening to set off a big blaze?

KEEP IT SHUT STUDY GUIDE

4. What is the most important lesson or fact about anger from this study that you want to allow to alter your thinking, your behavior, or your speech? How would you say it in a sentence? Once you have your sentence, program your phone or computer to send it to you a week or two from now. When it arrives, evaluate yourself to see if you have made any progress in this area.

Scripture Memory Verse of the Week

Here is this week's verse to ponder, study, and even memorize if desired. (Remember, all the memory verses are printed together at the back of this study guide. You may photocopy them for your convenience.)

> *"In your anger do not sin": Do not let the sun go down while you are still angry, and do not give the devil a foothold.*
>
> Ephesians 4:26–27

Session 6

AS SWEET AS HONEY: WONDERFUL WAYS TO USE YOUR WORDS

Gracious words are a honeycomb,
sweet to the soul and healing to the bones.

(PROVERBS 16:24)

Checking In (10 minutes)

Welcome to the final session of Keep It Shut. *Can you believe this is our last time together? An important part of this study is sharing what you have learned from reading the book and from completing your between-sessions personal study. Remember, you are still welcome at the study even if you weren't able to complete the material.*

- What from the session five video segment most challenged or encouraged you since the group last met? How did you fare in the area of not letting your anger morph into sin? Were you able to respond differently this time than you normally do?

- What insights did you discover from your reading of chapter 9 of the *Keep It Shut* book?

- What did you get out of the between-sessions personal study?

VIDEO: As Sweet as Honey: Wonderful Ways to Use Your Words (23 Minutes)

Play the video segment for session six. As you watch, record any thoughts or concepts that stand out to you in the outline that follows.

Notes

Psalm 139:1 – 5 tells us that before a word is even on our tongue, God knows it completely! The Amplified Version of the Bible brings forth the richer meaning of the original Hebrew words of this psalm: "You sift and search out my path and my lying down, and You are acquainted with all my ways. For there is not a word in my tongue [still unuttered], but, behold, O Lord, You know it altogether. You have beset me and shut me in — behind and before, and You have laid Your hand upon me" (vv. 3 – 5).

Both Ephesians 4:30 – 32 and James 1:21 beckon us to "get rid of" filth, evil, and all forms of unkind and unchristian behavior.

In order for us to get rid of such behaviors, sometimes we need a spiritual deadheading session with the Gardener of our soul.

Deadheading flowers is removing the faded blooms that are left clinging to the plant. If they are left on the stem, they sap the nutrition and strength from the core of the plant, preventing new growth from happening.

Sometimes having a visual reminder of the fact that we, as followers of Christ, are servants of God can help keep us from sinning with our words. Karen wears a toe ring. Others may pierce their ear or wear another piece of jewelry.

We become known for how we use our words. Barnabas was known as an encourager.

"Gracious words are a honeycomb, sweet to the soul and healing to the bones." (Proverbs 16:24)

The sweetness or bitterness of honey is determined by what the bee drinks in and the amount of time it spends in the sun.

The sweetness or bitterness of our words will be determined by what we drink in and the amount of time we spend with the Son.

Group Discussion (10 minutes)

Take a few minutes to discuss what you just watched.

1. What part of the teaching had the most impact on you?

2. What thoughts do you have on the concept from Psalm 139:1–5 of God knowing our words even before we speak them? How might recalling this truth help us to temper our language?

3. Do you have any experience with deadheading flowers or herbs? What can you tell the group about this process?

4. What are your thoughts about the reason why Karen wears a toe ring? Do you feel a visual reminder you wear on your body might enable you to keep the perspective that you are a voluntary servant of Christ? How might this help you watch your words? Are there any other ideas you can think of that might also help in maintaining such a perspective?

Cluster Group Discussion (8 minutes)

If your group is comprised of more than twelve members, consider completing this discussion in smaller groups of three to six people each.

5. Take turns reading aloud the two passages below. After each passage is read, list the various habits, actions, and sins it says we must rid ourselves of. Then discuss and record what we should be putting on instead (or what opposite behaviors we should be adopting).

   • Ephesians 4:30–32

   • James 1:21

   Which "get rid of" item spoke to you most, and why? What proper behavior or godly characteristic could you replace that item with?

6. Have someone read Paul's words to Timothy in 1 Timothy 6:20–21 and 2 Timothy 2:15–19. Listen for a repeated phrase that has to do with a type of speech Christians are to avoid.

What do you think "godless chatter" means? (Some translations call it "vain babblings," "irreverent babble," "empty speech," or "foolish, useless talk.")

A little investigation into the original meaning of the Greek words used for the phrase "turn away from (or avoid) godless chatter" reveals a more detailed snapshot of what Paul is urging Timothy to do. To "turn away from" connotes avoiding at all costs, planning ahead not to become involved, or remaining aloof. Perhaps these verses are telling us not only to avoid using this type of language but to stay far away from others who do.

"Godless chatter" means empty, with no meaning or purpose. However, there is another clue about what Paul may be referring to. Some translations mention the word "irreverent." This means not only what we think of when we hear the word today — dishonoring to God or his Word — but insinuates that a person might be using God or his commands in an improper manner to gain something. It might be money. Or attention. Or clout. Or to win an argument. Both times when Paul writes to Timothy about godless chatter, he also brings up false teachers who are infecting the church. This helps to paint a fuller picture of what godless chatter is and how we need to make sure it isn't coming from our mouths or entering our ears.

Knowing all this, what other guidelines can you think of for us today when obeying Paul's advice to Timothy? As a cluster group, craft one sentence that incorporates both the ideas of not using godless chatter and refusing to have any part in the irreverent babble of others. You will share this summarizing sentence with the larger group.

Group Discussion (10 minutes)

7. Have individual groups share the sentence they came up with that summarizes the Bible's instruction on avoiding godless chatter.

8. Have a few people read Proverbs 16:24 aloud in various translations. Then converse a little about the story of Karen interviewing Jake, the teenage beekeeper. How does knowing the process that makes honey sweet and abundant help you to better comprehend what makes our words sweet? How can sweet words also be healing, as mentioned in Proverbs 16:24? (In the medical world, honey is known for its anti-inflammatory and antibacterial properties, and has been used in previous ages to dress wounds.)

9. Of the many places we use our words — with our spouses, our kids, our extended family members, at work, with strangers, online, or with God — in which area do you most want to see improvement and change, so that your speech matches the directives in Scripture? What are your plans to propel this transformation?

10. Briefly review the notes you took in this study guide over the course of the group's time together and be ready to share one insight that really grabbed your attention. Then spend a few moments allowing those who wish to share their takeaway to do so.

Closing Prayer (2 minutes)

Have one person close in prayer, thanking God for the work he has done and the growth he has caused in each of your lives in knowing what to say, how to say it, and when to say nothing at all.

Also, be sure to discuss as a group if this will be your last session together, or if you will use bonus session seven to not only discuss your final personal study but also to have a little celebration, perhaps using some of the themed recipes provided.

FINAL PERSONAL STUDY

"So," I questioned my young friend, "Is it safe to say that the sweetness or bitterness of honey is determined by what the bee drinks in and the amount of time it spends in the sun?"

"Exactly!" he replied.

DING! DING! DING! We have a winner. I think I found my answer. Perhaps it is also true that the sweetness or bitterness of our words will be determined by what we drink in and the amount of time we spend with the Son.

Keep It Shut, page 203

Read and Learn

Read chapters 10–11 of the *Keep It Shut* book and record any thoughts or insights you discovered in the space provided.

Study and Reflect

1. Think back to your life before you started this study. On a scale of 1 to 10 (with 1 being "never" and 10 being "always"), what number would you have given yourself when it comes to how often your words lined up with the teachings of Scripture?

Has that number changed at all? Or do you have a desire to see that number change? Explain. (Hint: In order to really gauge this, look back at what you wrote for an answer in the "Individual Activity: What Is God Saying to Me?" at the end of the session one group time. Have you seen progress since then?)

> Let's not let the progress we've made together over our time together just melt away like a double dip of tutti-frutti left out on the picnic table on a hot summer's day. Let's aspire to use our mouths with godly purpose.
>
> To build ... not to break.
>
> To bless ... not to badger.
>
> To encourage ... not to embitter.
>
> To praise ... not to pounce.
>
> You with me? Good.
>
> *Keep It Shut*, page 203

2. Of all the stories, examples, Scripture passages, and group conversations during the course of the *Keep It Shut* study, which one has clung to your heart and mind in a Velcro-like manner? Why?

3. Take the next few days to think about the many areas in which you may be tempted to use your words in a wrong manner. Or to speak when you should keep your lips zipped. Or perhaps the opposite — to fail to speak up when you should. Choosing just one or two areas, write out your goals in the form of an honest prayer to God about each area. Be specific, mentioning situations, places, or people. (Or you may wish to use some sort of code or initials instead of an actual person's name, just in case your study guide falls into the hands of someone else.)

Area #1

Area #2

4. Read Proverbs 25:11. How has this study helped you learn to speak words that are "fitly spoken," "timely," or uttered "at the right time"? What guidelines might you set for yourself to ensure that your words are not only beautiful — "like apples of gold in settings of silver" — but also delivered at the most opportune time?

Scripture Memory Verse of the Week

Here is our last verse to ponder, study, and even memorize if desired. (Remember, all the memory verses are printed together at the back of this study guide. You may photocopy them for your convenience.)

> *Gracious words are a honeycomb, sweet to the soul and healing to the bones.*
>
> Proverbs 16:24

Also, take a minute now to review all six memory verses. Choose one that you want to make your goal to live out. If you have not already done so, post it in a prominent place where you will see it often. Read it. Ponder it. Memorize it. Live it.

Prayer of Commitment

Close this study by spending a few moments in prayer. Ask God to continue to guide you as you seek to be a woman after his own heart — a follower who is learning, step-by-step, to stop trying to control other people and circumstances and to trust him instead. Make this prayer time one of commitment to living life according to God's plan for you.

Final Note from the Author

Oh how I wish we were together face-to-face! As you finished your last day of this study, I would give you a hug and whisper my hopes to your heart.

I hope you don't let your mouth get you in as much trouble as mine has over the years.

I hope you will apply the biblical principles pointed out on these pages — the very ones that can restrain you from sinning with your speech.

I hope you speak life to others and impart courage to their souls.

I hope that when a family member's behavior threatens to knock the nice right out of you, you pause before you pounce.

I hope you make a habit, during the bumpy times of life, to hit your knees before you hit the phone (or tap away on the keyboard).

And I hope that long after this book has been placed on a shelf, passed on to a friend, or brought you a whole buck-fifty at your yard sale someday, that you'll still be reading the Book daily — God's go-to instruction manual for life.

Time for me to use my words one last time. This time as I have the privilege of praying for you. (See next page.)

Father, please bring to this sweet reader's memory what we've learned together during this study. Help her to know what it means to be angry but not sin. To not let the sun go down while she still harbors even a slight pinch in her heart toward anyone. To be quick to listen, slow to speak, and slow to become angry. May she make it her aim to give a soft answer, thereby helping to stop a family fight before it ever begins. Enable her to be selfless and humble rather than selfish and haughty. May she zip her lips when she knows she is beginning to gossip. Empower her to avoid godless chatter and instead speak only with a reverent purpose. May her words not become a spark that sets off a wildfire of regret. Help her to notice the one who least expects to be noticed, changing a life history with her encouraging words. May she build up and not break down. And most importantly, will you tap her on the heart and remind her of the truth that you see everything, Father? She so wants to please you. Will you help her to do just that? Assist her in keeping the lines of divine communication open. May she continue to learn how and when to keep her mouth shut while she keeps her heart wide open to you. In Jesus' name, amen.

Karen

BONUS SESSION

CELEBRATE WITH A WRAP-UP SEVENTH MEETING

Now that the six regular sessions have come to a close, your group might like to meet for one more bonus session as a wrap-up: to discuss the material you read after session six in chapters 10–11 of *Keep It Shut* as well as to celebrate your time together these past weeks.

In addition to discussion questions, session seven includes a few hands-on reflection activities and some yummy recipes to make your last session part study, part party! You'll notice several recipes have a honey theme in keeping with Proverbs 16:24: "Gracious words are a honeycomb, sweet to the soul and healing to the bones." Others are apple-based to remind us, "A word fitly spoken and in due season is like apples of gold in settings of silver" (Proverbs 25:11 AMP). For added effect, serve the food on silver platters — or at least silver-colored ones available at dollar stores.

Feel free to set the length of your bonus session. It can be anywhere from an hour to an entire slumber party!

IMPORTANT NOTE TO LEADERS:

If you add a bonus session seven, thoroughly read the session beforehand to coordinate the menu and food preparation and to purchase items as needed. You may wish to ask members for a suggested donation of a few dollars each to cover the cost of the materials of any activities or a take-home gift. Or if you are doing the study through a church, you may have money in the budget for these expenses.

Food: As noted, honey- and apple-themed recipes are included at the end of the bonus session. You may ask some group members to volunteer to bring any of these dishes. Or they may bring their favorite honey or apple dishes or search for new recipes online. You might even want to hold an apple or honey bake-off, where members bring dishes and everyone samples and votes on the best one. Perhaps the church staff is invited to blind taste-test dishes to select the winners. Winners get a prize! Or you may wish to keep the party simple and let a few women bring whatever munchies and beverages they desire, not keeping with any theme.

Gift: As a token and a reminder to watch their words, you might choose to give every group member one of the following items. Whenever she sees or uses it, she will be reminded of what she learned during the study time:

- Lip gloss or lip balm. (A honey-flavored lip balm such as Burt's Bees® brand would be especially appropriate in keeping with the Proverbs 16:24 theme of "gracious words are like a honeycomb.")

- A jar or bottle of honey.

- A bottle of iced tea sweetened with honey, such as Karen's favorite Sweet Leaf® brand Organic Mint & Honey. (Tie a ribbon around the neck of the bottle to dress it up.)

- Some actual honeycomb, usually found at farmers' markets or large grocery stores.

- A small bottle of honey- or apple-scented lotion, again with a ribbon to make it cute.

- A new toothbrush and a laminated note card with one of the verses from the study. (Women can tape the note card up to their bathroom mirror to study and memorize each day for a few minutes while they brush their teeth.)

- A set of laminated note cards with the six memory verses from the sessions to place in the shower to study and memorize. Remember, they are sized to fit in a business card holder, so you may wish to give them in one. (Maybe add a small bottle of apple- or honey-scented bodywash.)

- A journal and fancy pen to pen their words and prayers to God.

- A set of inexpensive note cards to use their words to bless others in their lives.

- A bag or box of alphabet pasta and a handwritten recipe card for alphabet soup.

- A box of alphabet shortbread cookies and an individual foil package of hot cocoa mix or coffeehouse gift card.

- A box of tea bags in a honey flavor such as honey-lemon or honey-and-mint, or an apple variety like apple-cinnamon.

- You may even want to give away one bigger door prize, such as a traditional board game that uses words — for instance, Scrabble, Boggle, Balderdash, Upwords, or Apples to Apples.

- Or you could make up an entire gift basket full of honey- and/ or apple-themed foods and items for a door prize.

Session 7

BONUS SESSION:
JUST GOTTA HAVE THE LAST WORD

Opener

For fun, play the old game of telephone. Write down a rather long and detailed paragraph that includes dates, numbers, multiple colors, names, etc. Then read it as a whisper into one person's ear. Have that person in turn whisper it to the next person, who will whisper it to the next one, and so on, going through at least ten people if you have that many. Then, for fun, see how close to the original the final message comes out.

Group Discussion

1. Since the group was last together, we read chapters 10–11 of *Keep It Shut*. Take a few moments to glance back over these chapters. Was there anything you highlighted, were struck by, or had a question about in chapter 10? Share your thoughts with the group.

   Was there anything you highlighted, were struck by, or had a question about in chapter 11? Share your thoughts with the group.

2. In chapter 10 of *Keep It Shut*, Karen tells about two incidents from her past where someone used words to bring either life or death. One involved a woman from a nearby church who encouraged Karen, saying, "I believe in you." The other involved two women at her college who told her, "We'd like you to lose a little weight," which Karen's heart interpreted as, "We would like you … *if* you would lose a little weight. If you don't, then we won't like you." Can you remember words or phrases that still resonate with you today because someone spoke either life or death? Share, but be careful not to use specific names or dishonor someone if you still feel a pinch in your heart over the incident.

Individual Activity: What Is God Saying to Me?

On your own, ask God to bring to mind someone who once said something hurtful to you. Perhaps it's a situation you still feel wounded by or that perhaps provokes anger, bitterness, or resentment when you think of it. Then, write briefly about the incident in the space provided.

Now take a moment to read this passage:

Therefore, God's chosen ones, holy and loved, put on heartfelt compassion, kindness, humility, gentleness, and patience, accepting one another and forgiving one another if anyone has a complaint against another. Just as the Lord has forgiven you, so you must also forgive. Above all, put on love — the perfect bond of unity.

Colossians 3:12 – 14 HCSB

What do you notice about these verses — especially the sentence about having a complaint against another?

Did you catch this important distinction? It does NOT read, "accepting one another and forgiving one another if anyone has a complaint against another *only if the person you have a complaint against totally and sincerely apologizes to you in person and asks for your forgiveness.*" OUCH! Instead, we are urged to forgive as the Lord forgave us. Even if you do not feel you should have (or could have) a face-to-face encounter with this person, would you take a few moments now in the space provided to write words of forgiveness to him or her anyway? Forgive as Jesus did — no matter the magnitude of the sin, from the heart, no strings attached. Remember what was mentioned in chapter 5 of *Keep It Shut*: "Unforgiveness is like sipping on poison and then expecting the other person to die" (page 92.)

Finally, ask the Lord to persistently nudge you if he wants you to extend forgiveness in person (or by letter, phone call, or email). This is not always necessary and may open old wounds or previous relationship tensions, especially if the other person never realized you were hurt or offended. Be careful and prayerful as you decide what to do.

Group Discussion

Gather as one large group again for the following questions:

3. The first question in the session six personal study was this: *Think back to your life before you started this study. On a scale of 1 to 10 (with 1 being "never" and 10 being "always"), what number would you have given yourself when it comes to how often your words lined up with the teachings of Scripture? Has that number changed at all?* Share your answers, if you are willing. And then open it up to talk a little about growth and accountability opportunities in this area.

4. As you look back over the book and study guide, what verses of Scripture have been most meaningful to you, and why?

5. Of the Bible characters covered in the book and study — Joseph, chapter 2; Daniel, chapter 4; David, chapter 7; and Herod, chapter 8 — did one particularly stand out as an example of how you should or should not use your words?

6. If you could pick just one concept, idea, story, warning, or encouragement from *Keep It Shut*, which would you be most likely be able to recall a year from now? Why do you think it impacted you so deeply?

Individual Activity: Note to Self

This activity was first suggested in the final chapter of Keep It Shut, *so there is a chance you may already have done it. If so, during this activity time, write an encouraging letter to someone who needs it, specifically pointing out aspects of his or her personality and character that you admire. If you'd like, use the "Love Prompts" (see sidebar on next page) as starters.*

Use the stationery and stamp provided by your leader to write a letter to yourself. Yes — to yourself. In it, encourage yourself with what you have learned from this journey. What do you need to work on? Why do you need to work on it? What relationships are being damaged, or precious time and memories lost, because of how you interact with those in your life, whether they are family, friend, or even foe? Spend a little time thinking about this and then let your pen and paper do the talking.

Write it out. Seal it up. Address it to yourself and affix a forever stamp to the front. Then, give it to your group leader. She will be praying about when she should pop it into the mail some time in the next year without you knowing. When the letter arrives, open it and read your own words. Hopefully, by God's grace and in his strength, you will have seen lasting progress in this important area.

LOVE PROMPTS

Got a minute? Grab a pen! Use any of these prompts to get you started on jotting a note, an email, or a text to a loved one in your life. For some, the statement stands alone. For others, elaborate on the thought that is given. Your words are sure to bless your recipient!

Five Powerful Phrases to Speak to Your Spouse

I trust your judgment.
I'm glad I married you.
Here is what I appreciate most about you …
I am with you.
Being your wife has taught me …

Five Powerful Phrases to Speak to Your Child

You can do it.
A happy memory I have of when you were younger is …
I am confident you can make good choices.
Being your mom has taught me …
God has an amazing life planned for you.

Five Powerful Phrases to Speak to Your Parent

I'm not sure if I've ever told you before, but thank you for …
A wonderful memory I have of my childhood is …
I admire your strength.
How can I help you?
I am proud of you for …

Five Powerful Phrases to Speak to Your Friend

My favorite thing about our friendship is …
The best time I ever had with you was when …
I am with you all the way.
The character quality I most admire in you is …
You remind me of Jesus when you …

Making a Pledge

Hopefully these past few weeks of intentionally looking at what the Bible says about how we are — and are not — supposed to use our words has prompted some lasting life and habit changes. If you are so led, tell the group what pledge you want to make when it comes to your words. Here are a few suggestions to get the ball rolling:

- I want to be more loving in the way I talk to my kids around home.

- I am going to try harder to speak respectfully to and about my husband (or boss or mother-in-law).

- I am going to really pray before I post words online, being more careful to watch my digital tongue.

- I want to get better at speaking the truth in love because I tend to be a people-pleaser and don't always tell the truth.

- I want to get better at speaking the truth in love because I tend to say what I think is the truth in an unloving manner.

- I don't want to be a gasoline queen anymore, throwing fuel on an already smoldering situation by escalating a family argument.

- I want to stop slinging my opinion and vow to give it only when directly asked.

Praying a Prayer

Have one member close the group in prayer and also pray a thankful blessing over the food you are about to enjoy. Or if you wish, you may have the women break into groups of two to four for closing prayer.

Let's Eat!: Recipe and Food Ideas

To help you get cooking, here are some of Karen's favorite dishes she makes for family and friends:

Appetizer

Caramel Apple Dip

Ingredients:

8 oz. cream cheese
1 t. vanilla
¼ c. sugar

¾ c. brown sugar
1 c. coarsely chopped salted peanuts

Blend all but peanuts until smooth. Add peanuts just before serving. Use with a tart eating apple, such as Granny Smith, Cortland, or Gala. If you must slice the apples long before eating them, soak slices in lemon-lime flavored pop to keep them from turning brown. Drain well and serve with the dip.

Main Dish

Herbed Honey-Lime Barbecued Chicken

One recipe of this sweet, sticky, and delicious chicken dish serves 6–7, so adjust according to how many people are in your group. Great with rice pilaf or a simple lettuce salad.

Ingredients:

12-oz. can tomato paste
½ c. olive oil
2 T. white or apple cider vinegar
2 T. mustard
⅛ c. real lime juice
½ c. brown sugar, firmly packed
¼ c. honey

1 t. dried basil
½ t. dried oregano
¼ t. garlic powder (or ⅛ t. fresh minced garlic)
¼ t. salt
¼ c. water
3 pounds boneless, skinless chicken breast strips

In a large bowl, mix all but chicken. Spray a slow cooker with cooking spray and place chicken in the bottom. Cover well with the sauce mixture. Cover and cook on low for 4–6 hours.

Side Dishes

Honey-Glazed Fruit Salad

Use your imagination with this one. Simply cut up 6–8 cups of assorted fruit. Toss with the homemade dressing. Add walnuts and ta-da! Delicious honey-glazed fruit salad. Serves 6.

Ingredients:

Dressing
⅓ c. honey
⅓ c. orange-pineapple juice
⅛ c. vegetable oil
juice of one lemon
2 t. poppy seeds (optional)
pinch of salt

Fruit/Nuts
diced tart apples with peel on (try Granny Smith, Fuji, Gala, or Honeycrisp)
chunked pineapple
sliced bananas
tangerine sections, halved
canned mandarin oranges, drained
red or green grapes
1 c. walnut pieces

Combine dressing ingredients and set aside. Cut fruit, place in a large bowl, pour dressing over the top, and toss well. Just before serving, add walnut pieces.

Honey-Glazed Baby Carrots

Slightly sweet and tender-crisp. Serves 4.

Ingredients:

1 lb. fresh baby carrots
2 T. honey

2 T. butter
pinch of salt

Steam carrots until tender, about 5–7 minutes. Place in a large bowl and toss with the remaining ingredients.

Bread

Serve your favorite corn bread muffin, whole grain bread slices, or chewy dinner rolls warm with this amazingly easy honey-butter on top. Yum! This recipe is enough for 16 people.

Cinnamon Honey-Butter

Ingredients:

2 sticks real butter, softened
½ c. honey
1 t. ground cinnamon

Mix all well and cover. Refrigerate. Before serving, take out and let stand at room temperature for an hour.

Desserts

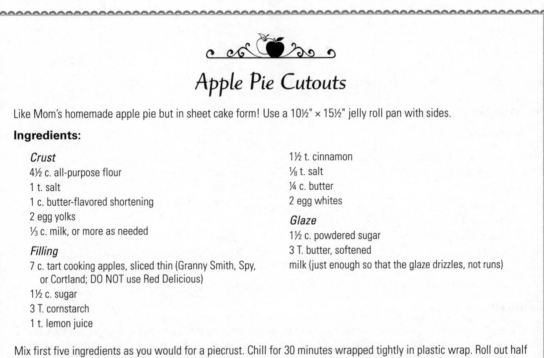

Apple Pie Cutouts

Like Mom's homemade apple pie but in sheet cake form! Use a 10½" × 15½" jelly roll pan with sides.

Ingredients:

Crust
4½ c. all-purpose flour
1 t. salt
1 c. butter-flavored shortening
2 egg yolks
⅓ c. milk, or more as needed

Filling
7 c. tart cooking apples, sliced thin (Granny Smith, Spy, or Cortland; DO NOT use Red Delicious)
1½ c. sugar
3 T. cornstarch
1 t. lemon juice

1½ t. cinnamon
⅛ t. salt
¼ c. butter
2 egg whites

Glaze
1½ c. powdered sugar
3 T. butter, softened
milk (just enough so that the glaze drizzles, not runs)

Mix first five ingredients as you would for a piecrust. Chill for 30 minutes wrapped tightly in plastic wrap. Roll out half of the dough and place on an ungreased cookie sheet.

For filling: Mix apples, sugar, flour, lemon juice, cinnamon, and salt. Spread evenly on crust; dot with butter. Roll out remaining dough on a lightly floured surface and place on top. Prick all over with a fork. Beat egg whites and brush on top. Sprinkle with a cinnamon/sugar mixture, if desired. Bake at 350 degrees for 35–40 minutes.

After removing from oven, cool completely and then glaze. Cut into squares for serving.

Honey-Lemon Poppy Seed Bread

As pretty as it is tasty!

Ingredients:

½ lb. (2 sticks) unsalted butter, softened

2½ c. granulated sugar, divided

2 T. honey

4 large eggs

¼ c. grated lemon zest

¾ c. freshly squeezed lemon juice, divided

¾ c. buttermilk

1 t. pure almond extract

3 c. all-purpose flour

½ t. baking powder

½ t. baking soda

1 t. salt

2 T. poppy seeds

Glaze

2 c. confectioners' sugar, sifted

3½ T. freshly squeezed lemon juice

dash of almond extract

Directions:

Preheat the oven to 350 degrees. Grease and flour two 8-inch loaf pans. With an electric mixer, cream the butter, 2 cups sugar, and honey in a large bowl until light and fluffy. Add the eggs, one at a time. Add lemon zest. Mix in ¼ cup lemon juice, the buttermilk, and almond extract.

Sift together the flour, baking powder, baking soda, and salt in a separate bowl. Combine the flour and buttermilk mixtures together, mixing until smooth. Stir in poppy seeds. Divide the batter evenly between the pans, and bake for 45–60 minutes or until a cake tester comes out clean. If the tops begin to brown too much, cover with pieces of foil gently set on top.

Combine ½ cup granulated sugar with ½ cup lemon juice in a small saucepan and cook over low heat until the sugar dissolves. Let loaves cool for 10 minutes. Remove from the pans and set them on wax paper or foil. Drizzle the lemon syrup over them. Let loaves cool completely.

For the glaze, combine the confectioners' sugar, lemon juice, and almond extract in a bowl, mixing with a wire whisk until smooth. Pour over the tops of the cakes and allow the glaze to drizzle down the sides.

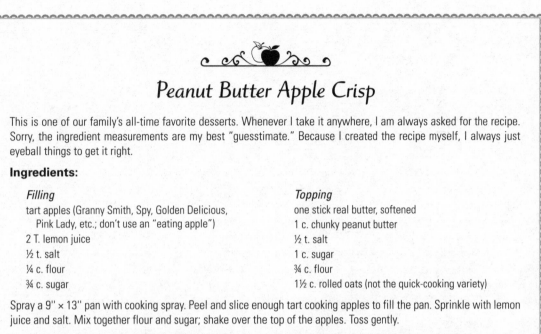

Peanut Butter Apple Crisp

This is one of our family's all-time favorite desserts. Whenever I take it anywhere, I am always asked for the recipe. Sorry, the ingredient measurements are my best "guesstimate." Because I created the recipe myself, I always just eyeball things to get it right.

Ingredients:

Filling

tart apples (Granny Smith, Spy, Golden Delicious, Pink Lady, etc.; don't use an "eating apple")
2 T. lemon juice
½ t. salt
¼ c. flour
¾ c. sugar

Topping

one stick real butter, softened
1 c. chunky peanut butter
½ t. salt
1 c. sugar
¾ c. flour
1½ c. rolled oats (not the quick-cooking variety)

Spray a 9" × 13" pan with cooking spray. Peel and slice enough tart cooking apples to fill the pan. Sprinkle with lemon juice and salt. Mix together flour and sugar; shake over the top of the apples. Toss gently.

For the topping, mix butter and peanut butter. Add in the next four ingredients. It should hold together in clumps when pressed in your fist. If it's too sticky, add a little more flour. Sprinkle topping over the apples and bake at 375 degrees for about 25 – 30 minutes, until apples are tender and topping is lightly golden. Serve with vanilla ice cream or whipped cream. FABULOUS!

ADDITIONAL
RESOURCES

Following is a collection of information, Scripture verses, and short quotes, excerpted from the book or study guide, to help enable you to know what to say, how to say it, and when to just *Keep It Shut*! Use this section as a go-to guide in the days ahead as you continue to strive to use your words for God's glory. As with the memory verses, you can cut them out, put them on card stock, and tape them where you'll see them regularly in your home, office, or car. Or type a few and put them in your smartphone or computer.

WHAT GOSSIP IS AND IS NOT

Gossip is:

- Divulging a secret we were specifically asked not to share.

- Divulging a secret that we are pretty sure is not meant to be shared, even if we weren't explicitly instructed not to repeat it.

- Telling a story about someone we have not yet verified to be true.

- Speaking about others in a way that paints them in a negative light so the listener will form an unflattering opinion.

- Talking in a cryptic way about someone, subtly suggesting something questionable or even scandalous about his or her character.

- Starting a story with a statement such as, "You know, they say …" "They" can speak for themselves. Quoting "they" as the source of a story is a red flag. "They" are the origin point of ginormous amounts of gossip.

Gossip is not:

- Processing a conflict or difficult situation between you and another person (or persons) with a trusted and tight-lipped friend, family member, mentor, counselor, or support group.

- Speaking words as straightforward facts, making no effort to cast the other person in a bad light.

- Seeking support, guidance, and prayer for handling the situation.

- Giving your honest opinion when asked about someone's character in a reference situation, such as when someone is applying for a job, a scholarship, or a leadership position.

- Giving your opinion about another person with words that impart grace, point out the honorable parts of his or her personality and character, and leave the less-than-lovely parts unsaid.

Don't say something permanently painful just because you are temporarily ticked off.

Advice from Proverbs:
- Don't speak too much.
- Don't speak too soon.
- Don't speak without first listening.
- Don't speak at all.

Words are powerful and they have consequences.

Make your speech laced with grace.

Hit your knees before you hit the phone (or the keyboard).

Believe the best before you assume the worst.

"Prayer will make a man cease from sin, or sin will entice a man to cease from prayer." — John Bunyan

Sticks and stones may break my bones, but words can never hurt me? No! Bruises fade and bones heal, but a scorched heart may take years to mend.

Mind your own sin, sweetheart.

Don't be a Gasoline Queen!

Are your words like a Snuggie®?

Hang on a second, I gotta die.

The sweetness or bitterness of honey is determined by what the bee drinks in and the amount of time it spends in the sun. Likewise, the sweetness or bitterness of our words will be determined by what we drink in and the amount of time we spend with the Son.

"Be wise in the way you act toward outsiders; make the most of every opportunity. Let your conversation be always full of grace, seasoned with salt, so that you may know how to answer everyone." (Colossians 4:5—6)

"They have become filled with every kind of wickedness, evil, greed and depravity. They are full of envy, murder, strife, deceit and malice. THEY ARE GOSSIPS." (Romans 1:29)

"Before a word is on my tongue you, LORD, know it completely." (Psalm 139:4)

"Do you see a man who speaks too soon? There is more hope for a fool than for him." (Proverbs 29:20 HCSB)

"The one who gives an answer before he listens — this is foolishness and disgrace for him." (Proverbs 18:13 HCSB)

"A soft answer turns away wrath, but a harsh word stirs up anger." (Proverbs 15:1 ESV)

"Even fools are thought wise if they keep silent, and discerning if they hold their tongues." (Proverbs 17:28)

"My dear brothers and sisters, take note of this: Everyone should be quick to listen, slow to speak and slow to become angry, because human anger does not produce the righteousness that God desires." (James 1:19 – 20)

"And do not grieve the Holy Spirit of God, with whom you were sealed for the day of redemption. Get rid of all bitterness, rage and anger, brawling and slander, along with every form of malice. Be kind and compassionate to one another, forgiving each other, just as in Christ God forgave you." (Ephesians 4:30 – 32)

"So get rid of all the filth and evil in your lives, and humbly accept the word God has planted in your hearts, for it has the power to save your souls." (James 1:21 NLT)

ADD YOUR OWN!

SCRIPTURE MEMORY VERSES

For your convenience, the memory verses for this study are printed here in the size of a standard business card. Feel free to photocopy this page on card stock and then cut out the verses. You can then purchase a portable business card holder to keep them in and carry them with you throughout your day. This way, you can memorize and practice reciting your verses in the carpool line, waiting room, on lunch hour — any time you have a few spare minutes. Be sure to check to see if any members of your group want to arrive early to the sessions to practice reciting the verses from memory for each other.

Session 1

*Hatred stirs up conflict,
but love covers over all wrongs.
Wisdom is found on the lips of the discerning.*

(Proverbs 10:12–13a NIV)

Session 2

*When there are many words,
sin is unavoidable, but the one
who controls his lips is wise.*

(Proverbs 10:19 HCSB)

Session 3

*My mouth speaks what is true, for my lips detest
wickedness. All the words of my mouth are just;
none of them is crooked or perverse.*

(Proverbs 8:7–8 NIV)

Session 4

*Instead, we will speak the truth in love,
growing in every way more and more like
Christ, who is the head of his body, the church.*

(Ephesians 4:15 NLT)

Session 5

*"In your anger do not sin": Do not let
the sun go down while you are still angry,
and do not give the devil a foothold.*

(Ephesians 4:26–27 NIV)

Session 6

*Gracious words are a honeycomb,
sweet to the soul and healing to the bones.*

(Proverbs 16:24 NIV)

Keep It Shut

What to Say, How to Say It, and When to Say Nothing at All

Karen Ehman

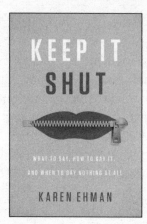

From Bible times to modern times, women have struggled with their words. What to say and how to say it. What not to say. When it is best to remain silent. And what to do when you've said something you wish you could now take back. In this book a woman whose mouth has gotten her into loads of trouble shares the hows (and how-not-tos) of dealing with the tongue.

Beyond just a "how not to gossip" book, this book explores what the Bible says about the many ways we are to use our words and the times when we are to remain silent. Karen will cover using our speech to interact with friends, coworkers, family, and strangers as well as in the many places we use our words in private, in public, online, and in prayer. Even the words we say silently to ourselves. She will address unsolicited opinion-slinging, speaking the truth in love, not saying words just to people-please, and dealing with our verbal anger.

Christian women struggle with their mouths. Even though we know that Scripture has much to say about how we are—and are not—to use our words, this is still an immense issue, causing heartache and strain not only in family relationships, but also in friendships, work, and church settings.

Available in stores and online!

Let. It. Go.: A DVD Study

How to Stop Running the Show and Start Walking in Faith

Karen Ehman

In this six-session video-based women's small group Bible study, Karen Ehman provides practical, biblically based steps for letting go of the need to control.

Let's face it: many women are wired to control. We make sure that the house is clean, the meals are prepared on time, the beds are made, the children are dressed, and everyone gets to work, school, and other activities on time. And trying to control it all is not only exhausting but can also cause us to lose friends and the affection of our families. It can earn wives and mothers the label of control freak and send those within our sphere of influence packing.

In this humorous yet thought-provoking small group Bible study, you'll find the freedom and reward of living "out of control"—putting God in the rightful place he deserves in your life. Armed with relevant biblical and current examples (both to emulate and to avoid), doable ideas, new thought patterns, and practical tools to implement, this study will gently lead you out of the land of over-control and into a place of quiet trust.

This DVD is designed for use with the *Let. It. Go. Study Guide* (sold separately). Sessions include:

1. God Called and He'd Like His Job Back
2. Combating the "Me First" Mentality
3. Pursuing the Appearance of Perfection
4. Practicing the Art of Soul Control
5. When Comparisons Lead to Over-Control
6. Fixing Your Eyes on the Attitude Indicator

Available in stores and online!